The Nature Kid's Guide to
PORCUPINES

DAVID ANDERSON

LP Media Inc. Publishing
Text copyright © 2026 by LP Media Inc.

For information address LP Media Inc. Publishing,
30012 Variolite St NW, Princeton MN 55371
www.lpmedia.org

Publication Data

Porcupines
The Nature Kid's Guide to Porcupines — First edition.

Summary: "Learn all about Porcupines, the Nature Kid Way"
— Provided by publisher.

ISBN: 979-8-89818-166-6

[1. Porcupines – Non-Fiction] I. Title.

Title: The Nature Kid's Guide to Porcupines

CONTENTS

FOREST FLOORS

Crunch! A porcupine waddles over dry leaves at dusk.

North American porcupines live in forests. They make homes in woods with many trees. Look for them in thick pine forests and shady oak woods.

These animals need trees all year long. They rest in rocky caves or small **dens**. Some hide under big roots or fallen logs.

A forest gives a porcupine everything it needs. Tall trees provide food to eat and cozy spots to rest. The forest floor is full of trails these slow walkers use night after night.

RANGE ROAM

FUN
FACT!
North American porcupines
have been found living at over
12,000 feet above sea level!

Rustle! A porcupine pushes through brush in a big forest.

Porcupines roam across a huge part of North America. They live from Alaska all the way down to Mexico. That is a lot of land to call home!

You can find them in Canada and most of the United States. Some live in cold, snowy places. Others live where it is warm and dry.

Porcupines do well in many types of land. Mountains, valleys, and flat plains all work for them. As long as there are trees or shrubs nearby, porcupines can make a home.

PUDGY PALS

The beaver is the only rodent in North America bigger than a porcupine!

Thump! A chunky porcupine drops from a low branch to the ground.

Porcupines are some of the biggest **rodents** around. A grown porcupine can weigh up to 35 pounds. That is as big as a lot of dogs!

From nose to tail, they can be three feet long. Most of that is their round, chubby body. The tail adds about eight more inches.

Males are a bit bigger than females. But all porcupines look pudgy and wide. Their thick coat of **quills** makes them look even bigger than they really are!

BODY BASICS
DID YOU KNOW?
A porcupine's front teeth are bright orange from a coating of iron that makes them extra strong!

Scratch! A porcupine digs its long claws into rough tree bark.

A porcupine has a round body and short legs. Its strong claws curve like hooks. Those claws help it grip trees and climb with ease.

Soft fur covers the belly and chest. Stiff, sharp quills line the top of the body and tail. A thick tail helps the porcupine balance on branches high above the ground.

Big front teeth sit at the front of its mouth. These teeth never stop growing! Chewing on wood keeps them from getting too long.

SNIFF STUFF

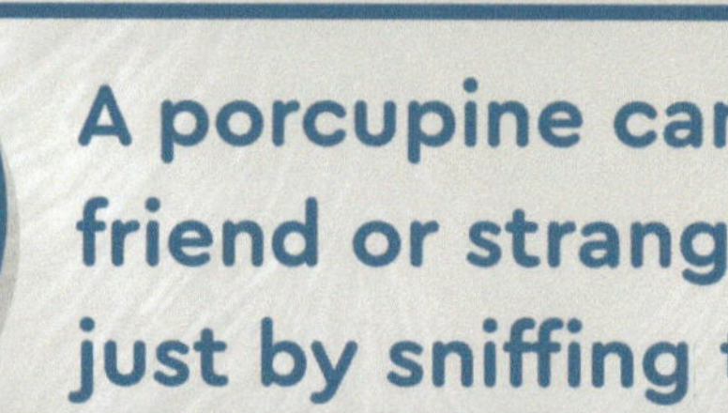

A porcupine can tell if a friend or stranger is near just by sniffing the air!

Sniff, sniff! A porcupine smells something yummy nearby.

Porcupines have a great sense of smell. They use their noses to find food in the dark. A porcupine can sniff out a tasty plant from far away.

Their eyesight is not very good. Things far away look blurry to them. But they do not need sharp eyes when their nose works so well!

Porcupines can also hear well. Their small ears pick up soft sounds in the night. Long whiskers on the face help them feel what is close by, even in total darkness.

POKEY PINS

Porcupines cannot shoot their quills — but the quills fall out so easily that it seems like they can!

14

Clack! A porcupine raises about 30,000 sharp quills on its back.

A porcupine has about 30,000 quills. Each quill is stiff like a needle. They cover the back, sides, and tail in a thick, spiky coat.

The tip of each quill has tiny hooks called **barbs**. These barbs stick into skin and are very hard to pull out. That is what makes quills so painful!

Quills are made of keratin — the same stuff as your fingernails. They lay flat when the porcupine is calm. But when scared, the quills stand straight up like a warning sign!

BARK
BITES

DID YOU KNOW?

A hungry porcupine can strip
a tree bare in one winter —
sometimes killing it!

16

Munch! A porcupine chews on a big strip of tree bark.

Porcupines love to eat bark. They strip it right off trees with their strong teeth. In winter, bark and twigs are their main meals.

When spring and summer arrive, they eat more greens. Leaves, clover, and berries are all yummy treats. Porcupines also munch on buds and flowers.

These animals crave salt like crazy! They will chew on old bones and antlers to get it. Some even nibble on wooden signs or tool handles that have salty sweat on them.

CHATTY CHAPS

FUN FACT!

Porcupines make over a dozen different sounds, including screams, moans, and grunts!

Eeee! A porcupine lets out a high whine in the dark woods.

Porcupines talk to each other with sounds. They grunt, click, and squeal. A baby porcupine makes soft whines to call its mother.

When a porcupine is mad, it chatters its teeth loudly. The sound says, "Stay away!" It might also stamp its feet and hiss to scare off trouble.

Porcupines use smells to talk too. They leave a strong scent on trees and rocks. Other porcupines sniff these marks and know exactly who has been there.

FIERCE FOES

DID YOU KNOW?
A fisher can take down a porcupine in less than 30 minutes by attacking its face!

Swoop! A great horned owl dives toward a porcupine. It almost falls out of the tree!

Even with sharp quills, porcupines still have enemies. The fisher is a small but fierce hunter. It can flip a porcupine on its back to reach the soft belly with no quills.

Great horned owls swoop down from above. Their strong claws can grab a porcupine right off a branch. Coyotes and mountain lions hunt them too.

Most hunters learn to leave porcupines alone. A face full of quills hurts a lot! But some hungry animals keep trying anyway.

STAY SAFE

A dog that gets quilled may have 500 quills stuck in its face — ouch!

Rattle! A porcupine shakes its quills and turns its back to danger.

When a porcupine spots danger, it does not run. Running would be pointless anyway — porcupines are too slow! Instead, it turns its back toward the threat so the quills face the enemy.

Next, it swings its thick tail. One hard smack can push dozens of quills into a nose or paw. That quick slap is very painful!

If trouble gets too close, the porcupine tucks its face down. It curls into a spiky ball. Most animals back away before getting poked.

CLIMB HIGH

Porcupines fall out of trees so often that one study found 35% had healed broken bones!

24

Scrape! A porcupine pulls itself up a tall pine tree slowly.

Porcupines are great climbers. Their curved claws dig into bark like hooks. Bumpy pads on their feet also help them grip the tree.

On the ground, porcupines walk in a slow waddle. They rock from side to side as they move. A porcupine is definitely not built for speed!

Surprisingly, porcupines are also good swimmers. Their hollow quills are filled with air. This helps them float on top of the water like a tiny boat.

NIGHT LIFE

DID YOU KNOW?

In winter, porcupines may come out during the day to warm up in the sun!

Hoot! An owl calls as a porcupine starts its nightly walk.

Porcupines are **nocturnal** animals. That means they sleep during the day and come out at night. As the sun sets, a porcupine wakes up hungry and ready to eat.

Most of the night is spent looking for food. A porcupine may climb a tree and feed for hours. It chews slowly and takes its time — there is no rush.

When the sky starts to get light, the porcupine heads back to its den. It finds a safe spot and curls up to sleep. Then it does it all again the next night!

SOLO STROLL

FUN FACT!

A porcupine's home area can cover 200 acres — that's about 150 football fields!

Shuffle! A lone porcupine ambles down a quiet forest path.

Porcupines like to live alone. Unlike wolves or deer, they do not travel in groups. One porcupine is perfectly happy by itself.

Each porcupine has its own home area. This is the patch of forest where it finds food and sleeps. Two porcupines may live close by but rarely see each other.

In cold winters, something changes. A few porcupines may share a den for warmth. But once spring comes, they go back to living on their own.

FALL FLINGS

FUN FACT!

Male porcupines spray smelly
liquid on females to impress
them — weird but true!

Waaah! A male porcupine howls into the cool fall night air.

Porcupines find mates in the fall. A male will follow a female for days. He howls and calls loudly to get her to notice him.

The male dances for the female. He stands up tall on his back legs and waves his paws in the air. He makes soft sounds to show he is friendly, not a threat.

After mating, the two part ways. The male goes off on his own again. About seven months later, a baby porcupine will be born.

PRICKLY PUPS

Squeak! A tiny porcupine snuggles with its mother in its log den.

Baby porcupines are called porcupettes. Most mothers have just one baby at a time. The baby is born in late spring or early summer.

A porcupette is born with soft quills that feel like wet noodles. Within a few hours, the quills start to harden. By the next day, the baby is already prickly!

Newborn porcupettes can see and walk right away. They weigh about one pound at birth. Even at that small size, they already look like tiny adults with big attitudes.

MAMA MOVES

DID YOU KNOW?
A mother porcupine calls
to her baby with soft
humming sounds at night!

Waddle! A young porcupine follows its mother out into the woods.

Mother porcupines take care of their babies alone. The father does not help at all. Mama feeds, guards, and teaches her porcupette all by herself.

The baby drinks its mother's milk at first. After just a few weeks, it starts to nibble plants too. The little porcupette learns what to eat by watching its mom.

By fall, the young porcupine is ready to live alone. It leaves its mother and finds its own home area. A porcupine grows up fast — in just five months!

SUPER QUILLS
DID YOU KNOW?
Some wild porcupines have lived
for more than 18 years!

Pop! A broken quill falls off and a brand new one grows in.

A porcupine's quills hold an amazing secret. Each quill has a special coating that helps fight germs. If a porcupine accidentally pokes itself, the coating helps it heal faster.

Lost quills grow back over time. It takes a few weeks for a new quill to push through the skin. This means a porcupine never runs out of its best defense!

In winter, porcupines have another trick. Their thick fur grows even longer to keep them warm. They may stay in one tree for days, munching bark and saving energy.

SPOT ONE!

FUN FACT!
You can sometimes smell a porcupine before you see it — they have a strong, musty odor!

Shhh! Look up in that tree and spot a sleeping porcupine.

Want to spot a porcupine? Look for signs in the trees! Stripped bark and chew marks on trunks mean one could be close by.

Check the ground for small, round droppings that look like brown beans. Porcupines also leave claw marks on tree trunks. These scratches show where they climbed up.

The best time to look is at dusk or dawn. Bring a flashlight and walk quietly. If you see a dark, round shape high in a tree, it might just be a porcupine resting until nightfall!

GLOSSARY

quills
Sharp, stiff spines that cover a porcupine's body.

barbs
Tiny hooks on a quill tip that stick into skin.

nocturnal
Active at night and sleeping during the day.

rodent
An animal with big front teeth that never stop growing.

den
A safe, cozy spot where an animal rests or sleeps.